Praise Notes

PRAISE NOTES

LEN WOODS

Tyndale House Publishers, Inc. Wheaton, Illinois

Produced by The Livingstone Corporation; David R. Veerman, project editor

Scripture quotations are taken from the *Holy Bible,* New International Version®. Copyright © 1973, 1978, 1984 by International Bible Society. Used by permission of Zondervan Publishing House. All rights reserved. The "NIV" and "New International Version" trademarks are registered in the United States Patent and Trademark Office by International Bible Society. Use of either trademark requires permission of International Bible Society.

ISBN 0-8423-2150-0

Printed in the United States of America

01   00 _99   98   97   96
7   6   5   4   3   2   1

FOREWORD

Praise Notes has been designed to help you learn to meditate on God's Word. Biblical meditation is not the "emptying" described by Eastern religion; rather, it is the filling of our minds with God's thoughts. Biblical meditation leads us to the renewing of mind that the Scripture directs in Romans 12:2.

Biblical meditation begins when we focus on bite-sized sections of God's Word. This allows us mentally to chew, digest, and receive spiritual nourishment and direction from the Scriptures. Biblical meditation helps us learn the depth of what God says by giving attention to the details of his Word. As a result, God's Word gets into us.

Praise Notes helps your biblical meditation in two ways. First, it limits the theme to what the Bible says about glorifying God.

Second, it places single verses or short texts before us for our attention, along with a sample meditation. Biblical meditation is the spiritual/mental conversation we have with God once we have invited his Word inside ourselves. May your conversations with the Lord transform your life.

Always put into practice what you learn. To help you do this, the phrase "Today I will praise God for" and a space for writing are included at the end of each meditation. Think about how you can apply what God is telling you, and write your action plan in the space provided.

For this reason a man will leave his father and mother and be united to his wife, and they will become one flesh.

GOD'S GIFT OF MARRIAGE

"Praise God for marriage!" No doubt some would read such a statement and respond, "What? Is that supposed to be a joke?" And the answer to that question is, "No, it's not *supposed* to be, but unfortunately it often is." Marriage is the fodder for sarcastic sitcoms. It is a perennial target for stand-up comics. Rather than viewing marriage as the holy institution that God intended it to be, our culture focuses on marriage as sinful people have distorted it. Don't let divorce statistics or horror stories sway you. This truth still stands: When a husband and wife determine by God's grace to live together in an unselfish fashion, they experience a blessing that is far above anything this world has to offer! And they present the world with a beautiful picture of the relationship between Christ and his church.

Today I will praise God for _____

_____

_____

*Then the man and his wife [Adam and Eve] heard
the sound of the Lord God as he was walking in the
garden in the cool of the day, and they hid from the
Lord God among the trees of the garden. But the
Lord God called to the man, "Where are you?"*

2

GOD'S PURSUIT OF SINNERS

Out of the terrible fact of humanity's rebellion in Eden comes
this truth: God never stops seeking out his sinful creatures. Over
and over the Scriptures portray God as pursuing and attempting

to reconcile fallen men and women to himself. Of course the ultimate expression of this divine search-and-rescue mission was the coming of Christ into the world for the purpose of seeking and saving "what was lost" (Luke 19:10). Take some time today to reflect on God's mercy and grace and how he worked in your life to bring you to himself.

Today I will praise God for _____

_____

_____

Then the Lord said to Abraham, "Why did Sarah laugh and say, 'Will I really have a child, now that I am old?' Is anything too hard for the Lord?"

GOD'S POWER

For a woman nearing ninety, the idea of first-time motherhood was a bit much—even if it was God making the promise. Sarah chuckled to herself at the thought. But God assured her that his words were no laughing matter—*nothing* is impossible with God. This truth is repeated time and again in the Scriptures (for example, see Job 42:2 and Luke 1:37). What "impossible" circumstances are you facing today? Instead of wringing your hands in resignation and despair, why not put your faith in a God who can do anything? He has unlimited power. As the psalmist says, "He does whatever pleases him" (Psalm 115:3).

Today I will praise God for _____

_____

_____

But Esau ran to meet Jacob and embraced him;
he threw his arms around his neck and kissed him.
And they wept.

God's Ability to Change Hearts

As Jacob approached Esau, he feared the worst, and for good reason. Years before, Jacob had used manipulation and outright deception to steal the special privileges and inheritance that rightly belonged to his older brother. Esau had vowed violent revenge. But over time, God transformed Esau's heart. Gone were the explosive anger and bitter jealousy. Instead, Esau grabbed his long lost "little" brother and bear-hugged him with great emotion. Don't underestimate God's ability to change anyone—even your most bitter enemy! God changes lives and heals relationships.

Today I will praise God for _____

_____

_____

*And now, do not be distressed and do not be angry
with yourselves for selling me here, because it was to
save lives that God sent me ahead of you. . . . So
then, it was not you who sent me here, but God.*

GOD'S SOVEREIGNTY

The story of Joseph is one of the clearest biblical examples of the
sovereignty of God. The Lord engineered a wild roller-coaster
sequence of events to get Joseph into position to care for his

family and thereby preserve the promise of the nation of Israel. Perhaps the most staggering aspect of the whole story is Joseph's response. He never complained. He never acted vengefully. Instead, he insisted that behind it all, and through it all, God had been in control.

In what areas of your life are you tempted to think that God has lost control? Instead of doubting, why not choose to trust? God controls the affairs of the universe and the details of your life.

Today I will praise God for _____

_____

_____

God heard their groaning and he remembered his covenant with Abraham, with Isaac and with Jacob. So God looked on the Israelites and was concerned about them.

$\mathcal{G}$OD'S MEMORY

Toiling under their Egyptian oppressors, the Israelites must have felt forgotten. At best, God was standing by, doing nothing. At worst, he had betrayed them and gone back on all his promises.

But the Scriptures reveal a different perspective. God heard their mournful prayers. He had *not* forgotten his covenant. He saw their plight and felt compassion. The very next chapter of Exodus reveals how God began to work to bring about their deliverance.

Though you may not always see it clearly, this truth is abundantly clear: God is aware of your pain and is faithfully watching, listening, and working in your life. Keep trusting!

Today I will praise God for _____

_____

_____

Moses' father-in-law replied, "What you are doing is not good.
You and these people who come to you will only wear yourselves
out. The work is too heavy for you; you cannot handle it alone.
Listen now to me and I will give you some advice."

GOD'S PROVISION OF WISE COUNSELORS

Moses' work as a judge was wearing him out. In trying to arbi-
trate all of the disputes of all the people of Israel, he was killing
himself and frustrating the masses. God sent wise counsel from

what many might consider a most unlikely source—his father-in-law. The counsel was simple: Delegate the work to competent representatives. When Moses followed this advice, everyone was better off.

God cares enough about us to do the same thing: He routinely sends people into our lives—friends, mentors, preachers, counselors—to share insights with us that, if heeded, will make our lives richer and more fulfilling. He provides wisdom through sermons, conversations, and books. Are your eyes and ears open to wise counsel today?

Today I will praise God for _____

_____

_____

Speak to the entire assembly of Israel and say to them:
"Be holy because I, the Lord your God, am holy."

GOD'S HOLINESS

The fact that God is holy means that he is absolutely pure. Since God is without sin and dwells in "unapproachable light" (1 Timothy 6:16), he cannot tolerate evil or even allow it in his presence. In the stern words of Hebrews 12:14, "Be holy; without holiness no one will see the Lord." Though the idea of God's holiness may seem daunting to woefully imperfect people, it can and should be seen in a positive light. A holy God can never treat us any way but perfectly. That news should fill our hearts with shouts of praise!

Today I will praise God for _____

_____

_____

Know therefore that the Lord your God is God; he is the faithful God, keeping his covenant of love to a thousand generations of those who love him and keep his commands.

$\mathcal{G}$OD'S FAITHFULNESS

There is perhaps no more beautiful word in the English language than *faithful*. It conjures up images of being trustworthy, reliable, dependable. One who is faithful can be counted on. You can bank on him or her. Such images are precisely what the Scriptures mean when they refer to God as a *faithful* God. We don't have to worry about whether he will come through. We don't have to wring our hands and wonder if he will really do what he has said he will do. In every situation, every day of our lives, God is faithful! He is always there for us!

Today I will praise God for _____

_____

_____

*The eternal God is your refuge, and underneath
are the everlasting arms.*

$\mathcal{G}$OD'S ETERNALNESS

Governments and galaxies come and go; men and millennia pass away. Though kingdoms rise and fall, and though the cosmos is gradually winding down, God endures. He has always been, and he will always be. Lovers of God can take comfort in the fact that God is eternal. He is without beginning or end. For finite creatures, the idea of an infinite Creator means stability and security. Since he holds time and space in his hands, surely he can take care of our lives. You are safe in his everlasting arms.

Today I will praise God for _____

_____

_____

For the word of the Lord is right and true;
he is faithful in all he does.

GOD'S TRUTHFULNESS

In an age marked by deception and distortion, it is difficult not to become a hardened skeptic. If we've been deceived or let down by someone, we usually end up being suspicious of others. And eventually, if we're not careful, such a wary attitude will even bleed over into the way we view the Word of God. "Can this really be true?" "Did God really mean this?" The sad result of such distrust is a powerless Christianity that neither fulfills us nor attracts others. We need to remember that God is true. Then, like Thomas the disciple, we need to "stop doubting and believe" (John 20:27). God is true, the very source of truth.

Today I will praise God for _____

_____

_____

The eyes of the Lord are on the righteous and his
ears are attentive to their cry.

GOD'S ATTENTIVENESS

Our world is loud and indifferent. Everyone clamors to speak;
few want to listen. For an overburdened heart, the need to be
heard is desperate and deeply felt. Perhaps that is where you find

yourself today—lonely and with no one to talk to. Or maybe you *do* have people you can actually talk to—they just don't listen to the words you say. Why not turn to the One who will never tune you out—God himself. He is watching, waiting, and listening!

Today I will praise God for _____

_____

_____

The Lord is close to the brokenhearted and saves
those who are crushed in spirit.

God's Nearness

God sometimes seems far away. We don't hear his voice. We don't see any hard-and-fast evidence of his working. Such dry times can leave us feeling confused and frustrated. And if we experience this sense of divine distance during an especially difficult time, we may even feel abandoned. But the clear testimony of Scripture is that God is continually near us—during both good times and bad. As Jesus put it, "I am with you always" (Matthew 28:20). In what specific ways would it change your daily experience if you began living as though God were right by your side? Honor God by trusting in the truth of his presence. As the psalmist wrote, "You will fill me with joy in your presence" (Psalm 16:11).

Today I will praise God for _____

_____

_____

PSALM 68:19

Praise be to the Lord, to God our Savior,
who daily bears our burdens.

14

$\mathcal{G}$OD'S CARE

In this song of praise, King David recalls God's great faithfulness to his people in overcoming their enemies. Tucked right in the middle of the psalm, this verse proclaims God's consistent compassion. He "daily bears our burdens." No wonder Peter, writing centuries later, urged his readers to "cast all your anxiety on him because he cares for you" (1 Peter 5:7). What burdens today do you need to roll onto the shoulders of the Lord? Give them to him, and praise him for his care! God always wants to help you.

Today I will praise God for _____

_____

_____

You guide me with your counsel, and afterward you will take me into glory.

GOD'S GUIDANCE

Good fathers guide their children, offering helpful advice and wise counsel. Their goal is twofold: They want to protect their offspring from harm, and they want to lead them into situations where they will experience blessing. Christians should not be surprised that this is also the way that God deals with us. If we read and obey God's Word, if we follow the leading of the Holy Spirit, and if we solicit the wise counsel of older, godly Christians, we can be confident that we will go in a way that will please God. Following such a path will help you avoid unnecessary heartache and will enable you to experience unbelievable blessings!

Today I will praise God for _____

_____

_____

As a father has compassion on his children, so the
Lord has compassion on those who fear him.

$\mathcal{G}$OD'S COMPASSION

Some Old Testament scholars note with interest the similarity
between the Hebrew words translated *compassion* and *womb*.
Their theory is that the word *compassion* may possibly be derived

from the warm and intimate feelings a loving mother has for the child developing within her womb. Is it possible to quantify such tender longings? Can mere words accurately convey such deep maternal affection? The compassion of God is like this—only to an infinite degree. Sometimes we may feel unloved and alone. But the truth is that God looks at us and at our predicaments and feels unlimited compassion! God tenderly and gently cares for you—he loves you.

Today I will praise God for _____

_____

_____

He makes grass grow for the cattle, and
plants for man to cultivate—bringing forth
food from the earth.

God's Gift of Food

It is common for God-fearing people to pause before meals, bow their heads, and pray. "Saying the blessing" we call it, or "returning thanks" or "saying grace." Whatever the phrase, the practice is entirely appropriate. Without food we would perish, and apart from God's provision, we would have no food. That's why Jesus had his disciples pray, "Give us today our daily bread." Contemplating these truths can help us avoid the common trap of "saying the blessing" in a rote, perfunctory way.

Today I will praise God for _____

_____

_____

Sons are a heritage from the Lord, children a reward from him. Like arrows in the hands of a warrior are sons born in one's youth.

GOD'S BLESSING OF CHILDREN

Solomon labeled children a "reward" from God. Unfortunately, screaming infants, meddlesome toddlers, and rebellious teenagers can cause us to lose sight of this truth. We may be tempted instead to view our children as a divine *punishment*. "What did I ever do, God, to deserve *this?*" Weary, frustrated parents need the encouragement of Psalm 127. Our children are "like arrows." Christian parents have the unique opportunity to teach them the truth about God and then shoot them out into a world that is desperate and dying. Don't despair, parent! You are involved in a task with eternal ramifications. Thank God for the opportunity to rear godly children!

Today I will praise God for _____

_____

_____

*Where can I go from your Spirit? Where can I
flee from your presence?*

$\mathcal{G}$OD'S OMNIPRESENCE

In this beloved psalm, David notes the fact that God is every-
where. Theologians call this God's *omnipresence*. Why is such a
doctrine significant to us? In hard times, it means God is always

with us, so we are never alone. In tempting times, it means we cannot escape the notice of God's watchful eye. In good times, it means we always have the privilege of enjoying God's presence no matter where we go. Just as God fills your life, so he fills the earth. Practice the presence of God today.

Today I will praise God for _____

_____

_____

He tends his flock like a shepherd: He gathers the lambs in his arms and carries them close to his heart; he gently leads those that have young.

$\mathcal{G}$OD'S GENTLENESS

In the midst of a chapter filled with references to God's vastness and majesty, we find this wonderful reminder of God's tenderness. If you can envision a kindly shepherd clutching a scared lamb close to his breast, then you're beginning to get the picture: God is like that with us. He is never harsh or violent or indifferent. Hundreds of years later, Christ would give an even clearer revelation of what Isaiah was saying: He is the Good Shepherd who always deals gently with his sheep. God gently leads you, corrects you, and cares for you.

Today I will praise God for _____

_____

_____

I will tell of the kindnesses of the Lord, the deeds for which he is to be praised, according to all the Lord has done for us—yes, the many good things he has done for the house of Israel, according to his compassion and many kindnesses.

21

GOD'S KINDNESS

The prophet Isaiah primarily spoke words of stern judgment. His message to the nation of Judah could be summarized this way: God is going to punish you for your rampant unfaithfulness. Yet,

Isaiah insisted, because of God's infinite kindness, his people would not be completely abandoned. Judah could look forward to a bright and hopeful future.

God has not changed. He still longs to care for us in a gentle and compassionate way. Take some time today to list the ways God has demonstrated his kindness to you.

Today I will praise God for _____

_____

_____

The Lord appeared to us in the past, saying: "I have loved you with an everlasting love; I have drawn you with loving-kindness."

GOD'S LOVE

The fact that God is loving shouldn't be surprising. According to 1 John 4:8, God's very nature is love. The fact that God is loving *to us,* however, ought to stagger us! There is nothing about us or in us to merit such loving-kindness—God simply chooses to shower us with his perfect and unending affection. The Christians who are most attractive and effective in this life are those who never get over the love of God. Ask God to give you a fresh sense of how deeply he cares for you. God loved you while you were yet a sinner and before you ever had a loving thought toward him.

Today I will praise God for _____

_____

_____

Who is a God like you, who pardons sin and forgives the transgression of the remnant of his inheritance? You do not stay angry forever but delight to show mercy.

23

God's Mercy

What is mercy? Mercy is being spared punishment. It means not having to face the awful consequences that we really deserve to face. Because of his perfect mercy, God devised a way by which we could avoid having to pay for our sins. God took our sins and our guilt and put them all on Christ. Then Christ took our punishment. Because God's justice was satisfied in the death of his Son, he is now able to offer us forgiveness, a pardon—or we might say *mercy.* An offer of mercy is a wonderful gesture, but it does no good until we accept it. Have you accepted God's offer of mercy?

Today I will praise God for _____

_____

_____

The Lord is good, a refuge in times of trouble.
He cares for those who trust in him.

GOD'S GOODNESS

One of the great struggles of the Christian life is maintaining confidence in God's goodness. This has been the case since the beginning of time. In the perfect environment of Eden, the devil came to Adam and Eve and slyly implied that perhaps God was *not* good. Why else, the serpent suggested, would he keep the first couple from tasting the forbidden fruit? Instead of listening to the deceptive accusations of the enemy, we need to commit ourselves to the biblical truth of the goodness of God. It is true, regardless of what we might think or feel.

Today I will praise God for _____

_____

_____

I the Lord do not change.

$\mathscr{G}$OD'S IMMUTABILITY

Everything about our world—the weather, laws, ideas, politics, fashions, trends, even people—is in a constant state of flux. Finding any long-term sense of security amidst such continual change and confusion is an exercise in futility . . . until we turn to the Lord. He is the one and only constant in all the universe. The fact that our God is, in the words of the writer of Hebrews, "the same yesterday and today and forever" (13:8) gives us confidence. We know where we stand. We can rejoice that as believers we have a solid anchor in what is otherwise a very shaky world. God is reliable and trustworthy, and he never changes.

Today I will praise God for _____

_____

_____

Blessed are those who hunger and thirst for righteousness, for they will be filled.

God's Satisfaction of Spiritual Desires

According to Jesus, our genuine desires for spiritual growth will never go unmet. If we truly want to know God and if we are desperate enough to pursue him at any cost, we will find satisfaction. This is a tremendous promise. It is the offer of a spiritual oasis to those who are spiritually hungry and thirsty. If you have experienced (or are presently enjoying) this kind of supernatural satisfaction, thank God for his goodness to you. If not, keep seeking God. In time you will find him, and he will meet the deep desires of your soul.

Today I will praise God for _____

_____

_____

This, then, is how you should pray: "Our Father in heaven. . . ."

$\mathcal{G}$OD'S FATHERHOOD

Jesus taught his disciples to view God as their heavenly Father. One great drawback to this analogy is the fact that most people project the characteristics of their imperfect earthly dads onto

God. Consequently, if your father was stern and aloof, the odds are great that you will tend to view God in the same way. No wonder one of the chief projects of the Christian life is coming to accurately understand the fatherhood of God! It is a lifelong exercise, but the place to begin is with God's perfection. Our divine Father always deals with us in perfect love, perfect patience, perfect fairness, and so on and so forth. Take the best father you have ever seen, subtract his failings, multiply his good qualities by infinity, and you begin to get the picture!

Today I will praise God for _____

_____

_____

Come to me, all you who are weary and burdened,
and I will give you rest.

$\mathcal{G}$OD'S REST

Invitations, depending on who sends them, what is offered, and when they arrive, can seem like godsends. A lonely person thrills in the unexpected invitation to a concert. The couple strapped for cash rejoices over their invitation to dinner at a friend's home. If those kinds of offers excite us, how much more should we rejoice in Christ's invitation to come to him for rest! The promise is clear: Tired, burned-out people can find an otherworldly peace in the arms of the Savior. The Lord Jesus Christ promises rest to all those weary and burdened who turn to him. That's an invitation that no other can match.

Today I will praise God for _____

_____

_____

But Jesus immediately said to them: "Take courage! It is I. Don't be afraid."

GOD'S ENCOURAGEMENT

The disciples were tired from a long day of ministry. They were frustrated by their inability to traverse the Sea of Galilee. Suddenly terror seized them. Through the mist they saw a spooky figure walking on the water, coming right toward them! The "ghost" was, of course, Jesus. And when he saw their emotional turmoil, he immediately spoke words of encouragement.

Are you tired, frustrated, or short of courage? Let the Savior comfort you. Take some time today to listen to his voice.

Today I will praise God for _____

_____

_____

*His master replied, "Well done, good and faithful
servant! You have been faithful with a few things; I
will put you in charge of many things. Come and
share your master's happiness!"*

GOD'S EXALTATION OF THE FAITHFUL

In this story, told near the end of his earthly ministry, Jesus gave
some clues about what the future would hold for his followers.
We don't have a lot of details, but this passage and others in the

New Testament clearly teach that all believers will one day stand before Christ (2 Corinthians 5:10). There our lives will be examined, and we will be rewarded according to how faithfully we have served the Lord. Such passages ought to motivate and encourage us. No act of service goes unnoticed—God sees. And eventually God will reward us for living for him. One day, God will reward your faithfulness.

Today I will praise God for _____

_____

_____

Indeed, the very hairs of your head are all numbered. Don't be afraid; you are worth more than many sparrows.

31

$\mathcal{G}$OD'S CONCERN

A receding hairline. A dead sparrow in the weeds behind your house. According to the Scriptures, the fact that God takes note of these insignificant details means that *nothing* is trivial to God; he is aware of even the smallest aspects of our lives. Why then do we worry? Why do we fear the unknown? We can trust in our good God who is vitally concerned with everything that affects us—both good and bad. God knows the details of your life and also is concerned with your well-being.

Today I will praise God for _____

_____

_____

I no longer call you servants, because a servant does not know his master's business. Instead, I have called you friends.

GOD'S FRIENDSHIP

It is easy to think of ourselves as God's creatures or even as his servants, but his *friends?* It is a staggering thought! How can unholy, imperfect, finite people become the close companions of a holy, perfect, infinite God? By the reconciling work of Jesus Christ. He came to die in our place, to pay for our sins, so that we might be brought back into a right relationship with God. The Father has taken the initiative, Christ has done all the work, and the Spirit beckons us to come. And yet it is only when we put our faith in the finished work of Christ that the offer of divine friendship becomes a reality. Do you know God as your Creator, Lord, and Friend? God has made it possible for you to be on friendly terms with him—because of the sacrifice of Jesus Christ.

Today I will praise God for _____

_____

_____

Then Peter began to speak: "I now realize how true it is that God does not show favoritism but accepts men from every nation who fear him and do what is right."

*G*OD'S IMPARTIALITY

Try as we may *not* to play favorites, we have a tendency to be partial toward certain people. We tend to ignore the nondescript child and gravitate, instead, toward the cute, precocious toddler.

We are (just barely) civil toward socially inept people even as we gush over those who are attractive and witty. In every part of our lives we have these tendencies. Fortunately for us, God does not show preferences. God does not play favorites—he is an equal-opportunity Creator! God accepts us, not on the basis of anything we are or do, but on the basis of who Christ is and what he has done for us. How does it make you feel, Christian, to know that God accepts you as much as he does his own Son?

Today, I will praise God for _____

_____

_____

Now to each one the manifestation of the Spirit is given for the common good.

GOD'S GIFTS

Much discussion (and even more conflict) has surrounded the biblical doctrine of spiritual gifts. But this much is clear: God has given every believer at least one gift. And when those supernatural endowments are used to build up the rest of the body, God works in miraculous ways! Instead of complaining about the gifts you do not possess or comparing yourself to others, why not thank God for graciously equipping you to serve a vital role in the building of his kingdom? Remember, God has given you unique gifts and abilities to use to serve the body of Christ, and gifts are for giving!

Today I will praise God for _____

_____

_____

Praise be to the God and Father of our Lord Jesus Christ, the Father of compassion and the God of all comfort, who comforts us in all our troubles.

$\mathcal{G}$OD'S COMFORT

If anyone had occasion to know the reality of divine comfort, it was the apostle Paul. His grocery lists of trials (2 Corinthians 6:4-10; 11:23-28) make the typical modern-day Christian experience seem like an extended stay at Disneyland! Yet with genuine, heartfelt emotion, Paul voices his gratitude to God for providing an undeniable sense of consolation and reassurance—even during the worst of times. When hard times come, do you wallow in complaint or rest in the comfort that God stands ready to provide? God's comfort equals or exceeds every trial that you will ever face.

Today I will praise God for _____

_____

_____

He has delivered us from such a deadly peril,
and he will deliver us. On him we have set our hope
that he will continue to deliver us.

$\mathcal{G}$OD'S DELIVERANCE

The same Greek word that appears in our Bibles as *save* is sometimes translated "deliver." In many instances it refers to spiritual salvation from sin and death, but sometimes, as in the case of 2 Corinthians 1:10, it carries the idea of physical deliverance from evil or suffering. Though the apostle Paul endured a number of difficult trials in his life, he also had many experiences where God "delivered" him from angry mobs, deadly illnesses, and natural disasters. We need to take comfort in the fact that our God is able to keep us from harm! God has delivered you in the past, and he will do so in the future.

Today I will praise God for _____

_____

_____

I will be a Father to you, and you will be my sons and daughters, says the Lord Almighty.

GOD'S ADOPTION

Salvation would be wonderful enough if it consisted solely of forgiveness. But salvation involves so much more than that. We are granted eternal life, indwelt by the Holy Spirit, placed into the body of Christ and—hold on to your hat—*actually, literally* adopted by God into his forever family! Imagine that—when we put our trust in Christ, we are granted the privilege of becoming God's children! This truth has the potential to radically change the way we live from day to day. Spend some time today meditating on your true identity as a son or daughter of the living God.

Today I will praise God for _____

_____

_____

So I say, live by the Spirit, and you will not gratify the desires of the sinful nature. . . . Since we live by the Spirit, let us keep in step with the Spirit.

GOD'S INDWELLING SPIRIT

Loving our enemies. Staying pure in an impure world. Holding our tongues. Being unselfish. Taking the gospel to a hostile world. These are just five of the monumental job assignments that God has given Christians. And the New Testament lists hundreds more. Is it possible for you—for *anyone*—to obey even a portion of these commands? Yes. We can live the Christian life, but only if we allow the Spirit of God to flood our lives and fill us with his power. As we follow his leading and rely on his strength, we are able to do things that are supernatural. Living by the Spirit is the way the impossible Christian life becomes possible.

Today I will praise God for _____

_____

_____

*In him we have redemption through his blood,
the forgiveness of sins, in accordance with the riches
of God's grace.*

God's Forgiveness

Pretty much everyone—from the wisest seminary professor to the youngest Sunday school student—can tell you that God hates sin. But often overshadowed by the holy judgment of God is the twin truth of his desire to forgive our sins. As you read the Scriptures, you get the distinct idea that God is as bothered by humanity's lostness as he is by humanity's sinfulness. So he stands ready, even eager, to forgive our rebellious attitudes and wrong choices. God's incomparable forgiveness is made available through the death of Jesus on the cross. When we admit our offenses, he sweeps them away like a cloud (Isaiah 44:22) and cleanses us (1 John 1:9). If you have experienced that kind of divine pardon, you know there's no greater feeling in the world. If you haven't, God longs to forgive you today! Why not ask him?

Today I will praise God for _____

_____

_____

In him and through faith in him we may approach
God with freedom and confidence.

$\mathcal{G}$OD'S ACCEPTANCE

Picture yourself in the presence of a rich, famous, or powerful person. How do you feel? Intimidated? Starstruck? Tongue-tied? Now picture yourself in the very presence of almighty God. What do you do? Cower? Cover your eyes? Fall on your face? In Ephesians, the apostle Paul cites the many blessings we have been given in Christ. One is the fact that because of the death of Christ on our behalf, we have the privilege of coming into God's presence with freedom and confidence! We are loved and accepted. Is this how you approach God? He loves and accepts you unconditionally in Christ.

Today I will praise God for _____

_____

_____

For this reason, since the day we heard about you,
we have not stopped praying for you and asking
God to fill you with the knowledge of his will
through all spiritual wisdom and understanding.

GOD'S IMPARTATION OF WISDOM

The apostle Paul understood that Christians need more than to be merely intelligent, knowledgeable, or "bright." A high IQ isn't enough. Human insight won't do. When it comes to living skillfully (and in a way that pleases God), we need wisdom from above. So Paul prayed that his friends in Colosse would come to possess such divine understanding. Perhaps he had read the great promise written by James, "If any of you lacks wisdom, he should ask God, who gives generously to all without finding fault, and it will be given to him" (James 1:5). Isn't it wonderful to know that we have access to this kind of higher education? God wants to direct your life and teach you the best way to live.

Today I will praise God for _____

_____

_____

All Scripture is God-breathed and is useful for teaching, rebuking, correcting and training in righteousness, so that the man of God may be thoroughly equipped for every good work.

42

GOD'S WORD

Without the Bible we would know only the vague truths about God revealed through nature. Apart from the Scriptures, we would have little sense of how to enter into a relationship with

God or what he expects of his children. But thank God that he *has* spoken and that he has preserved his words and his will for the ages. We do not have to guess or wonder about how he wants us to live. We must simply read, believe, and obey his eternal Word. This week, treat the Bible as the divine road map that it is.

Today I will praise God for _____

_____

_____

For the grace of God that brings salvation has appeared to all men.

God's Grace

Grace. Through the centuries, learned theologians and just regular folks have tried to understand it and explain it: "unmerited favor"; "getting what we don't deserve"; "God's riches at Christ's expense."

None of these noble efforts fully does justice to the term. As fallen creatures, the best we can hope for is an occasional glimpse of the truth. Even though we only see "a poor reflection as in a mirror" (1 Corinthians 13:12), what we witness in those moments of revelation is truly amazing. The truth is, God gave us all the blessings of salvation when he owed us nothing at all except judgment for our sin. Therefore grace is worth telling others about and thanking God for—no matter how feeble and clumsy and inadequate our words might be.

Today I will praise God for _____

_____

_____

Nothing in all creation is hidden from God's sight.
Everything is uncovered and laid bare before the
eyes of him to whom we must give account.

44

GOD'S OMNISCIENCE

The word *omniscience* comes from two Latin words—*omni,*
meaning "all," and *scientia,* meaning "knowledge." In other
words, to say that God is omniscient is to assert that he knows

everything. Not only all the things that have happened and will happen but also every possible event—past, present, and future. God is fully aware of everything in the universe and everything in our lives. God's omniscience should be wonderfully comforting—especially when coupled with the truths of his goodness and power. It brings new meaning to the old television show title *Father Knows Best*.

Today I will praise God for _____

_____

_____

By faith we understand that the universe was formed at God's command, so that what is seen was not made out of what was visible.

GOD'S CREATION

Creation *ex nihilo*—that's the fancy phrase theologians use to describe the fact that God created the entire cosmos out of nothing. Think of it! Using absolutely no raw materials, God called into being atomic elements, built them into molecules, and then began producing all that we see. Because of God's creative genius, we witness sunsets that can move us to tears, storms that can scare us out of our socks, and animals that can make us fall down laughing. Open your eyes today and study the wonders of creation. Then honor your magnificent Creator.

Today I will praise God for _____

_____

_____

So we say with confidence, "The Lord is my helper;
I will not be afraid. What can man do to me?"

*G*OD'S HELP

What a blessing to get help when we are in trouble! A good
Samaritan helps you get your car started. A neighbor watches
your children when you have to leave the house suddenly. A

fellow church member brings over a meal when you are under the weather. With so many caring folks around us, sometimes we lose sight of the one behind all those seemingly random acts of kindness—God himself—the ultimate Helper. Perhaps James, the brother of our Lord, said it best: "Every good and perfect gift is from above, coming down from the Father" (James 1:17). God is faithful to help you in your troubles.

Today I will praise God for _____

_____

_____

For you know that it was not with perishable things such as silver or gold that you were redeemed from the empty way of life handed down to you from your forefathers, but with the precious blood of Christ, a lamb without blemish or defect.

47

God's Provision

Some people read the Old Testament and complain that the Bible is a bloody book. "Why all the animal sacrifices? Was that really necessary?" The simple answer to those questions is "Because of the holiness of God and the sinfulness of humans, yes, there had to be judgment." Lambs were slaughtered daily to make fellowship with God possible . . . until Christ, the perfect Lamb of God, bled and died on a Roman cross. With that ultimate sacrifice, God's righteous anger regarding sin was satisfied for all time. That means a rich relationship with God is now possible—and all because of the "precious blood of Christ."

Today I will praise God for _____

_____

_____

The Lord is not slow in keeping his promise, as some understand slowness. He is patient with you, not wanting anyone to perish, but everyone to come to repentance.

48

GOD'S PATIENCE

In discussing God's judgment of sinners, the apostle Peter emphasized God's perfect patience. We witness and experience this divine attribute all the time. Others do terrible things that deserve swift punishment, yet they seem to get away with them. Though we know better, we often wander away from God, playing the prodigal. No lightning bolts fall. Doesn't God care? Perhaps he's sleeping. No. God sees it all. And he never ceases to be holy. But set against his hatred for sin is his patience. God mercifully puts up with your sin and foolishness. Let this truth motivate you to live in a way that honors God.

Today I will praise God for _____

_____

_____

Dear friends, now we are children of God, and what we will be has not yet been made known. But we know that when he appears, we shall be like him, for we shall see him as he is.

GOD'S PLAN

In this verse, the apostle John echoes a common scriptural theme: God's plan for our lives is to make us into Christlike people. This is not mere cosmetic change but deep transformation. This process is made difficult by several obstacles. Something *within* us stubbornly resists divine changes. Meanwhile, worldly ideals and spiritual forces *without* try to shape us into ungodly people. Praise God for the promise that, ultimately, nothing can thwart his plan to remake and renew us! God is conforming you to the likeness of his Son (Romans 8:29).

Today I will praise God for _____

_____

_____

All the angels were standing around the throne and around the elders and the four living creatures. They fell down on their faces before the throne and worshiped God, saying: "Amen! Praise and glory and wisdom and thanks and honor and power and strength be to our God for ever and ever. Amen!"

GOD'S WORTHINESS

In this heavenly scene, we are given a glimpse of what true praise looks like. The angelic creatures, who themselves are glorious beyond words, fall on their faces before the throne of almighty

God. In unison they thunderously proclaim the greatness and majesty of the Lord. If that is how God is honored in heaven, shouldn't we seek to glorify him on earth in much the same way? Ask God to reveal himself to you. When you see God as he is, you, too, will honor him with unceasing praise.

Today I will praise God for _____

_____

_____